IS-120.A: Introduction to Exercises

By

Fema

1/23/2008

Lesson 1: Exercise Basics

Lesson Introduction

After completing Lesson 1, you will be able to:

* Distinguish between different exercise types.
* Identify the main goals for conducting exercises.
* Describe the building block approach to exercises.

This lesson contains four topics followed by a video activity and a quiz:
Topic 1: Reasons for Conducting Exercises
Topic 2: The Building Block Approach
Topic 3: Discussion-Based Exercises
Topic 4: Operations-Based Exercises
Video Activity
Lesson Quiz

Reasons for Conducting Exercises

Key Concept: Exercise
(n) Something performed or practiced in order to develop, improve, or display a specific power or skill.
(v) To practice in order to train, strengthen, or develop.
 —Merriam-Webster's Dictionary

Exercises improve readiness by:

* Providing a way to evaluate operations and plans.
* Reinforcing teamwork.
* Demonstrating a community's resolve to prepare for disastrous and catastrophic events.

"We did not anticipate that airliners would be commandeered and turned into guided missiles; but the fact that we practiced for other kinds of disasters made us far more prepared to handle a catastrophe that nobody envisioned."
 —Rudolph W. Giuliani, former mayor of New York City

Quick Tip: Different people define "exercise" in different ways. To some, it means training and drills. To others, it's a way to evaluate and confirm the soundness of policies and procedures, through in-depth discussion. An exercise can be all of these-and more.

Reasons for Conducting Exercises

Main Goals

Exercises also help:

- Clarify roles and responsibilities.
- Improve interagency coordination.
- Find resource gaps.
- Develop individual performance.
- Identify opportunities for improvement.

The Building Block Approach

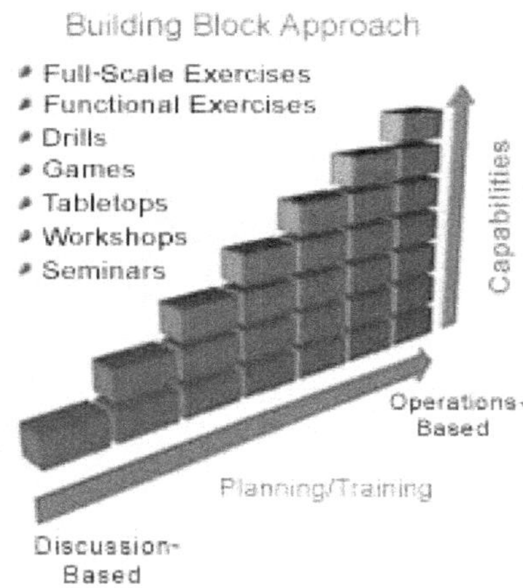

Exercises may range widely in cost, size, scope, complexity, purpose, and approach.

Key Concept: Exercises should be planned in a cycle that increases in complexity. Each successive exercise should build on the scale and experience of the previous one.

Building Block Parts

There are seven accepted types of exercises in the building block approach. Each exercise type falls into one of two categories. The two categories of exercises are Discussion-based exercises and Operations-based exercises.

Key Concept: Discussion-based exercises, as the name suggests, center on participant discussion.

Key Concept: Operations-based exercises focus on action-oriented activities such as deployment of resources and personnel.

The most basic exercise type in the building block approach is the seminar, which involves brief discussions of preparedness strategies and goals.

At the other end of the spectrum, the most complex, full-scale exercises can involve thousands of participants in responder gear, using equipment, trucks, evacuation routes, and actors, to simulate real emergency procedures.

Discussion-Based Exercises

These types of exercises:

- Provide a forum for discussing or developing plans, agreements, training and procedures.
- Are generally less complicated than operations-based types.
- Typically focus on strategic, policy-oriented issues.
- Include seminars, workshops, tabletops, and games.
- Do not involve deployment of resources.

Quick Tip: A facilitator or a presenter usually leads the discussions in these exercises, helping to keep participants on track and ensuring that exercise objectives are met.

Seminars

Key Concept: A seminar is an informal discussion-based exercise led by a presenter or facilitator, used to teach or orientate participants.

Goals

In a seminar:

- Orientate participants to new or existing plans, policies, or procedures.
- Research or assess interagency capabilities or inter-jurisdictional operations.
- Construct a common framework of understanding.

Conduct Characteristics

- Casual atmosphere.
- Minimal time constraints.
- Lecture based.

Workshops

> Key Concept: A workshop is a formal discussion-based exercise led by a facilitator or presenter, used to build or achieve a product.

Goals

In a workshop, participants:

- Develop new ideas, processes, or procedures.
- Develop a written product as a group in coordinated activities.
- Obtain consensus.
- Collect or share information.

Conduct Characteristics

- Involves more participant discussion than a lecture-based seminar.
- Often uses break-out sessions to explore parts of an issue with smaller groups.

Quick Tip: Products that are often produced from a workshop include: Emergency Operations Plans (EOPs), Mutual Aid Agreements, and Standard Operating Procedures (SOPs). Findings from the workshop should be collected into a short After-Action Report (AAR) and distributed to all parties involved. The AAR for workshops act much like meeting minutes and will be discussed in more detail later in this course.

Tabletop Exercises

> Key Concept: A tabletop exercise (TTX) involves senior staff, elected or appointed officials, or other key personnel in an informal group discussion centered on a hypothetical scenario.

Goals

In a TTX, participants:

- Identify strengths and shortfalls.
- Enhance understanding of new concepts.
- Seek to change existing attitudes and perspectives.

Conduct Characteristics

- Requires an experienced facilitator.
- In-depth discussion.
- Slow-paced problem solving.

Quick Tip: The purpose of a TTX is to test existing plans, policies, or procedures without incurring the costs associated with deploying resources. A TTX also allows participants to thoroughly work through a problem without feeling as much pressure as they would in an operations-based exercise.

Game

> Key Concept: A game is a simulation of operations using rules, data, and procedures designed to depict an actual or assumed real-life situation.

Goals

In a game, participants:

- Explore the processes and consequences of decision-making.
- Conduct "what-if" analyses of existing plans.
- Test existing and potential strategies.

Conduct Characteristics

- Does not involve the use of actual resources.
- Often involves two or more teams.
- Includes models and simulations of increasing complexity as the game progresses.

Quick Tip: A list of gaming products can be found at the Lessons Learned Information Sharing site, https://www.llis.dhs.gov/user/login.

Operations-Based Exercises

These types of exercises:

- Involve deployment of resources and personnel.
- Are more complex than discussion-based types.
- Require execution of plans, policies, agreements, and procedures.
- Clarify roles and responsibilities.
- Improve individual and team performances.
- Include drills and both functional and full-scale exercises.

Drills

Key Concept: A drill is a supervised activity that tests a specific operation or function of a single agency.

Goals

In a drill, participants:

- Gain training on new equipment.
- Test new procedures.
- Practice and maintain skills.
- Prepare for more complex exercises.

Conduct Characteristics

- Immediate feedback.
- Realistic but isolated environment.

Functional Exercises

Key Concept: A functional exercise (FE) is a single or multi-agency activity designed to evaluate capabilities and multiple functions using simulated response. In the past, FEs have occasionally been referred to as Command Post exercises (CPXs).

Goals

In an FE, participants:

- Evaluate management of Emergency Operations Centers, command posts, and headquarters.
- Assess the adequacy of response plans and resources.

Conduct Characteristics

- Simulated deployment of resources and personnel.
- Rapid problem solving.
- Highly stressful environment.

Quick Tip: Note the differences between drills and functional exercises:

- Drills involve a single function; FEs involve multiple functions.
- Drills involve actual deployment of resources and personnel; FEs use simulation.

Full-Scale Exercises

> Key Concept: A full-scale exercise (FSE) is a high-stress multi-agency, multi-jurisdictional activity involving actual deployment of resources in a coordinated response, as if a real incident had occurred.

Goals

In an FSE, participants:

- Assess plans and procedures under crisis conditions.
- Evaluate coordinated responses under crisis conditions.

Conduct Characteristics

- Mobilization of units, personnel, and equipment.
- Stressful, realistic environment.
- Scripted exercise scenario.

Activity Background

Choosing an Exercise Type

Jim and Mary work in the Jonesville emergency management office. They're trying to decide which exercises they should conduct this year.

[Mary and Jim sitting at table]

Jim: Hey, Mary. I've been looking over the after-action reports from last year's exercises. They were all chemical agent drills and functionals, which is fine, but I think Jonesville is ready to take it to the next level. We've addressed many of the action items from last year's exercises, we've purchased all the equipment we need, our teams are trained and we've got our plans in place. Now it's time to put everything into action.

Mary: What are you thinking?

Jim: Something more complex. Something using the 2 new chemical plants as a staging ground… We need something with victim role play, actual decon, triage, treatment, and transport to the local hospitals. We also need to involve the state's new regional response teams.

Mary: Do you really think we're ready for that kind of effort? You're talking at least 10 different departments… [Mary pondering the difficulty] We'd have to simulate an incident at one or both plants, coordinate multi-agency plans and communications, and get trucks, teams, and responders all at the same scene... That's a lot to handle.

Jim: Yeah, we're up for it! For two years the fire department has been building a great hazmat response team, the police department's last evacuation drill went off without a hitch; and I know our hospitals have spent a lot of time working on the decon processes, lately. What we haven't seen are all these groups working together with their boots on the ground - and they're going to have to if there's a major incident at one of the plants, so let's work those kinks out now.

Summary of Lesson 1

You have covered the following topics in Lesson 1:

- The purpose of conducting exercises.
- The benefits of conducting exercises.
- The building block approach.
- Types of discussion-based exercises.
- Types of operations-based exercises.

Lesson 2: Exercise Program Management

Lesson Introduction

After completing Lesson 2, you will be able to:

- Define exercise program management.
- Describe the Multiyear Training & Exercise Plan.
- Describe how exercises build capabilities.

This lesson contains three topics, a video activity, and a quiz:
Topic 1: Exercise Program Management
Topic 2: Multiyear Training & Exercise Plan
Topic 3: Capability Building
Video Activity
Lesson Quiz

Program Management

Defining Exercise Program Management

An exercise program provides the administration, supporting resources, and strategic goals for an organization's exercise efforts.

Key Concept: Exercise program management involves developing and executing an exercise program. This includes:

- Multiyear training and exercise program planning.
- Budgeting and grant writing.
- Planning and executing individual exercises.
- Tracking improvements.

Exercise program management can vary in size and scope, with staff members responsible for all or parts of these duties.

Quick Tip: Any organization, city, state, or federal agency may establish and manage an exercise program.

Multiyear Training & Exercise Plan

A multiyear training & exercise plan:

- Takes stock of current program plans and capabilities.
- Lays out long-term program goals and objectives.
- Develops a mix of exercises to meet goals and objectives.
- Determines what training is needed as a prerequisite to planned exercises.
- Sets a multiyear schedule of exercises.
- Sets a multiyear schedule of training events.

Quick Tip: The Multiyear Training & Exercise Plan is developed at a Training and Exercise Plan Workshop (T&EPW). The T&EPW usually occurs once a year and brings together key exercise personnel from all area agencies to discuss a program's strategy and scheduling of exercise and training for the coming year.

Multiyear Training & Exercise Plan

Multiyear Training and Exercise Schedule

Multiple, connected exercises that take place over time are called an exercise series.

Coordinating a program's various exercises and exercise series is a crucial part of a Multiyear Training & Exercise Plan.

Program managers use the Multiyear Training and Exercise Schedule to:

- Avoid duplicating their efforts.
- Combine exercises and ensure the exercises don't conflict.
- Combine training and ensure training does not conflict.
- Optimize and combine funding where possible.

- Prevent "over" training and exercising.

Quick Tip: Many series may be simultaneously occurring at any time within a program.

Capability Building

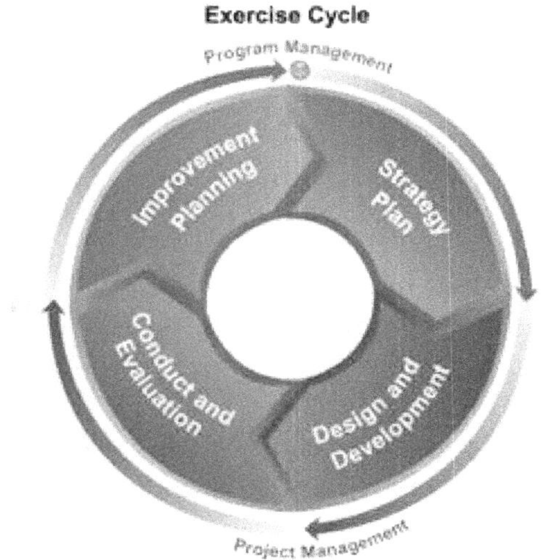

Program managers use exercises to build and improve upon an organization's capabilities. Validating training, plans, and equipment is a critical part of capability building.

Program managers should be continually evaluating exercise lessons to:

- Assess the adequacy of current training, plans and equipment.
- Prepare for future training, plans and equipment.
- Identify other resources needed to fill in capability gaps.

Activity Background

Multiyear Exercise Plan

Jonestate is conducting an Exercise Plan Workshop to schedule exercises around the state and its regions for the next three years. Stakeholders from different agencies and organizations sit in the audience and participate.

[Bill, the exercise planner, is standing at white board. Exercise Planning Workshop members Mary, Kristen, Jerry, and Frank are sitting at the table.]

Bill: Ok, that'll do it for July – let's get the August exercises up on the board. As we know there's a REP exercise at the nuke plant on the 12th. Who else has exercises planned?

Jim: Bill on the 10th, Mary and I were talking about putting on a full-scale at the Jonesville chemical plants. We want to build on the lessons learned from last year's exercises there.

Kristen: Bill [Kristen looking at her notes] CDC is planning on a Public Health tabletop in McIntosh county on the 25th. We also have a point of dispensing drill on the 12th with Gray and Henry counties.

Jerry: [raising hand and talking] Bill – the state's also doing a regional hurricane exercise on the 5th.

Bill: [Bill writing on white board.] Frank, anything from ODP?

Frank: Yup. [Frank looking at notes] We've got a local intel seminar in Hutchinson on the 10th. A multi-local Emergency Alert System drill on the 30th in Beauregard county and a pandemic flu tabletop in Jackson county on the 21st.

Bill: [Bill writing and looking at calendar.] That last one comes really close to the CDC tabletop in McIntosh. Why don't we take a look and see if they have similar objectives. And maybe we can combine some of these exercises.

Lesson Summary

This lesson covered the following topics:

- Exercise program management.
- The Multiyear Training & Exercise Plan.
- The Multiyear Training and Exercise Schedule.
- How exercises build capabilities.

Lesson 3: Establishing the Foundation

Lesson Introduction

After completing Lesson 3, you will be able to:

Identify the key components of exercise project management.

- Describe the critical aspects of an exercise planning team.
- Name the different types of exercise planning conferences.

This lesson contains three topics, a video activity and a quiz:
Topic 1: Exercise Project Management
Topic 2: Exercise Planning Team
Topic 3: Planning Conferences
Video Activity
Lesson Quiz

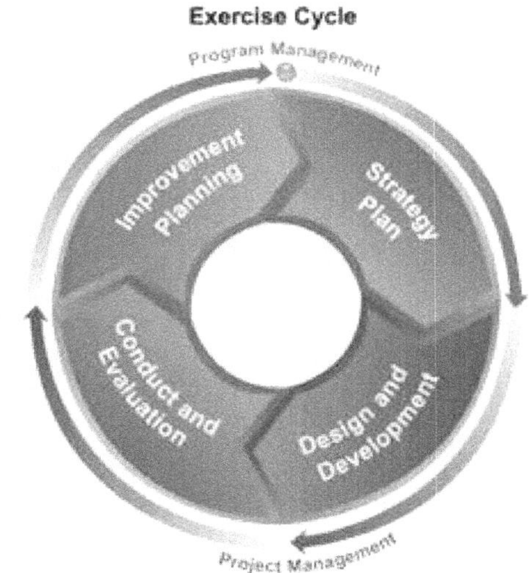

Defining Exercise Project Management

Key Concept: Exercise project management is the next step after program management. In this step, project managers are responsible for the design, development, and execution of a specific exercise, followed by evaluation and improvement planning.

Good project management involves:

- Developing a project management timeline.
- Establishing project milestones.
- Identifying the exercise planning team.
- Scheduling planning conferences.

These tasks are the foundation of every exercise - without them, other tasks and stages of the exercise planning cycle could not happen.

Quick Tip:

- Exercise program management = coordination of multiple exercises
- Exercise project management = coordination of an individual exercise

Exercise Project Management

Exercise Timeline

In program management, the Multiyear Exercise Schedule provides a long-term calendar for multiple exercises.

> Key Concept: In project management, the Exercise Timeline identifies key conferences and tasks for an individual exercise.

Exercise project managers build timelines to include:

- A schedule of key conferences and milestones.
- A Master Task List.
- Planning team task assignments.

Generally, timelines for discussion-based exercises are shorter and have fewer tasks than timelines for operations-based exercises.

Quick Tip: Often times, especially for larger exercises, exercise planning teams are set up much like the Incident Command System (ICS). When this happens, tasks are divided by function. However, depending on the size and resources available to plan the exercise, individuals may be assigned to tasks the project manager decides best matches their capabilities.

Exercise Planning Team

Key Concept: Every exercise requires an Exercise Planning Team - the core group responsible for the design, development, conduct, and evaluation of an exercise.

A team consists of a Lead Planner and planning team members.

The Exercise Planning Team:

- Determines exercise objectives.
- Creates the scenario.
- Develops exercise documentation.
- Conducts pre-exercise briefing and training sessions.

Because of their high level of involvement, planning team members are ideal selections for exercise controller and evaluator positions. As a general rule, however, they do not participate as players.

Quick Tip: The Lead Exercise Planner, (aka the Exercise Director) has complete management responsibility, assigning tasks to team members and ensuring the successful execution of the exercise.

Membership and Size

The Exercise Planning Team should be assembled from key participating agencies, organizations and jurisdictions. The scope and type of exercise or scenario should also help determine the team's membership.

For example, a "point of dispensing" drill that simulates the distribution of pharmaceutical supplies should involve planners and subject-matter experts from the medical and public health communities.

Consistent with NIMS/ICS principles, the team's size should be manageable and flexible - capable of expanding or shrinking, given the demands of the timeline and its associated tasks.

Quick Tip: Lead planners should consider planning team members as strong candidates for the positions of exercise controller and evaluator, but not as player-participants in the exercise.

Planning Team Organization

Task assignments are often based on the following functions:

- Command.
- Logistics.
- Operations.
- Administration/Finance.
- Planning.

These functions form the core of the Incident Command System (ICS) - a standardized method for managing emergencies. Planners use the ICS structure because it creates a distinct chain of command and accountability that ends with the Lead Exercise Planner.

Quick Tip: For example, using the ICS structure, the Logistics lead would be responsible for securing the planning conference and exercise site facilities, equipment, and communications. The Finance lead would identify and monitor all costs related to the exercise, and provide procurement and accounting plans.

The number of planning team members can vary depending on the functions or tasks involved in an exercise. The organization chart below shows a clear difference in personnel requirements between small- and large-scale exercises.

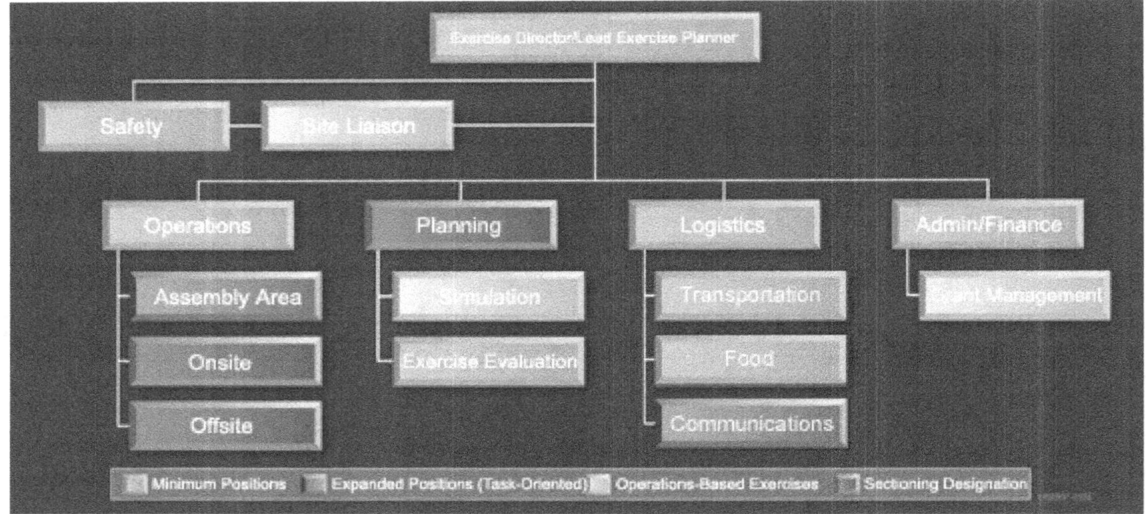

Quick Tip: For further information on the ICS, see the FEMA Independent Study Course, IS-700: National Incident Management System: An Introduction.

Planning Conferences

Key Concept: Planning Conferences are the official meetings held by the planning team to develop and coordinate an exercise.

The conferences provide an opportunity for the team to:

- Define the exercise purpose and objectives.
- Develop the scenario.

- Coordinate logistics.
- Track design and development progress.
- Troubleshoot design or development problems.

The scope, type, size, and complexity of the exercise determine the type and number of conferences the planning team decides to conduct.

Quick Tip: Discussion-based exercises typically require fewer planning conferences (between one and two), while operations-based exercises generally require more (between three and five).

Types of Planning Conferences

Five different types of planning conferences or meetings may occur during the planning process.

Concept and Objectives (C&O) Meeting

- Optional—may be rolled into the Initial Planning Conference (below).
- Exercise type, scope, scenario, and objectives are identified.
- Official Exercise Planning Team selection occurs.
- Sponsoring agency and senior officials attend.

Initial Planning Conference (IPC)

- If there is no C&O meeting, the IPC has the same characteristics, as well as the following.
- Refines exercise scope, scenario, and objectives.
- Solidifies exercise timeline and task list.
- Sets task assignments for planning team members.

Mid-Term Planning Conference (MPC)

- Settles outstanding logistical or organization issues.
- Site walkthrough is conducted.
- Usually only held for operations-based exercises.

Master Scenario Events List (MSEL) Conference

- Develops (or continues developing) scenario injects for exercise conduct.
- Usually only held for operations-based exercises.

Final Planning Conference (FPC)

- Final drafts of exercise materials are completed.
- Logistics and procedures for exercise conduct are finalized.
- Last opportunity to settle outstanding issues.

Activity Background

Assigning Tasks

Jim is leading the Initial Planning Conference for the Jonesville Chemical FSE.

[Jim, Mary, John, Josh, Molly, Paul, and Reese are sitting at the table.]

Voice Over: The Multi-year Exercise Plan that was developed out of the EPW in February calls for the conduct of a full-scale exercise at the Jonesville chemical plants. Based on the date of the exercise, set in August, some design and development milestones were also scheduled, such as the Initial Planning Conference.

Jim: Alright – just to recap thus far - so we're all clear on the goal of the exercise: we're going to be looking at a multi-agency response to a chemical release at the two new plants. [The planners nodding in agreement] Our primary objective is to examine the establishment and functionality of an incident command and unified command and specifically how they coordinate communication and response at the strategic and tactical levels.

Mary: [Mary looking at a list of major agencies] And we're all agreed that our key participating agencies should be the sheriff's office and state police for law enforcement; fire; HazMat; EMS; public affairs; the 911 dispatch center, hospitals, public health, the state EMA, regional response teams, and the chemical plants' response assets. [Mary looking back at participants] And of course, we're going to invite lots of others, but [Mary motions to the board] these players will be central to meeting our objectives.

Jim: Ok, so that's what we've covered thus far – now let's get down to task assignments [The planners pick up their notepads and pens]. John– I'd like you to handle Safety. Josh – you are in charge of logistics. Molly – you have the actor task list. Paul – why don't you take care of media and public information. And Reese – you've got exercise documentation.

Now we're going to do a detailed break down of tasks for each of these areas, but you'll be in charge of divvying out responsibilities for each – and following through on what you have delegated and to whom you have delegated those tasks….

Lesson Summary

This lesson covered the following topics:

- Project Management.
- Exercise Timeline.
- Exercise Planning Team Responsibilities.
- Planning Conference Types.

Lesson 4: Design and Development

Lesson Introduction

After completing Lesson 4, you will be able to:

- Define four key elements in the design and development of an exercise: scope, purpose, objective, and scenario.
- Understand the purpose of exercise documentation.

Defining Design and Development

Think of design as the framework of an exercise, and development as the building of that exercise.

Exercise design includes:

- Assessing exercise needs.
- Defining the scope of the exercise.
- Writing a statement of purpose.
- Defining exercise objectives.
- Creating a scenario for the exercise.

Exercise development includes:

- Creating exercise documentation.
- Arranging logistics, actors, and safety.
- Coordinating participants and media.
- Other supporting planning tasks (e.g., training controllers, evaluators, and exercise staff).

Needs Assessment

The best way to determine the appropriate exercise design is to assess your organization's (or jurisdiction's) capability needs.

A comprehensive exercise program will already have evaluated its organization's capabilities. Referring to and updating that assessment is an important step whenever a new exercise is considered for development.

The needs assessment will identify:

- Functions most requiring rehearsal.
- Potential exercise participants.
- Existing exercise requirements and capabilities.
- Plausible hazards and the priority levels of those hazards.

For example, if your jurisdiction has recently updated their Emergency Operations Plan, that plan should then be validated. Therefore, your needs assessment should reflect the desire to design and conduct an exercise which would then test that plan.

Scope

Like "exercises", the word scope has multiple interpretations.

> Key Concept: Most often, scope defines the kind, rather than the number, of exercise participants (i.e., levels of government/private sector).

Other interpretations include:

- Geographic size (local, national, regional).
- Number of participants.
- Responder functions.
- Hazard Type.

Exercise planners must be careful to make their scope manageable (neither too large nor too complex), selecting only those participants or actions best suited for the exercise program, type, budget, and objectives.

Purpose and Objectives

Purpose

Key Concept: An exercise's purpose statement is a broad statement listing the desired goals of the exercise.

The purpose of an exercise should be captured in a simple phrase that communicates the intent of the exercise. It does not describe in detail how the intent will be achieved.

Example of a purpose statement:
"This exercise is designed to provide feedback on the proficiency of the tasks involved in critical emergency response operations. It is also a learning opportunity for responders to examine the unique aspects of responding to chemical incidents."

Objectives

Key Concept: An objective is a description of the performance you expect from participants. It conveys specifically how the exercise should achieve its purpose.

Objectives:

- Define specific exercise goals.
- Provide a framework for scenario development.
- Provide exercise evaluation criteria.

Generally, the number of exercise objectives should be limited to enable timely execution, facilitate design of a reasonable scenario, and promote successful completion of the exercise purpose.

Use the SMART acronym to define objectives.

S imple	Don't try to cover too broad an area.
M easurable	Ensure evaluators can determine whether the objective was achieved.
A chievable	The objective should not be too difficult to achieve.
R ealistic	The objective should present a realistic expectation of the situation.
T ask-oriented	The objective should focus on a behavior or procedure.

Examples of objectives:

Discussion-based objective:

- Evaluate the standard operating procedure (SOP) for presumptive agent identification.

Operations-based objective:

- Assess the capability of the local hazardous material team to detect, identify, monitor, and respond to the effects of an unknown chemical release.
- Examine the abilities of the local response agencies to implement a large-scale decontamination of a mass casualty incident.

Scenario

Key Concept: A scenario is the storyline that drives an exercise.

It has three basic elements:

- General context or comprehensive story.
- Technical details of story's conditions and events.
- Conditions for assessing/demonstrating capabilities.

Scenarios should be:

- Threat-based and performance-based.
- Realistic.
- Challenging—but not so demanding that participants become overwhelmed.

A scenario should involve the participants, the threat and the area identified in the scope.

Scenario narratives should be designed to engage exercise participants in a way that approximates real-world responses to emergencies.

At a minimum, the narrative should address these questions:

- Where does the initiating event take place?
- How dangerous and persistent is the emergency?
- What is the impact of the incident?
- What time of day does the event take place?
- What is the sequence of events?
- What other factors would influence emergency procedures?

Exercise Documentation

Exercise documents are the most tangible elements of design and development. Different exercise types require different documentation. They may range from simple sign-in sheets to media releases and exercise evaluation guides.

The Exercise Planning Team is responsible for producing exercise documentation. The Lead Planner assigns responsibility for each document to individual members or groups.

Quick Tip: For examples and templates of exercise documentation, go to the HSEEP Volume IV Library.

Situation Manual
A Situation Manual (SITMAN) is the participant handbook for discussion-based exercises. It provides background information on the scope, schedule, and objectives for the exercise. It also presents the scenario narrative for participant discussions during the exercise.

Exercise Plan
The Exercise Plan (EXPLAN) is the participant handbook for operations-based exercises. The EXPLAN provides controllers, evaluators, players, and observers with information such as the exercise purpose, scope, objectives, and logistical information.

Controller Evaluator Handbook
Controller Evaluator (C/E) Handbooks supplement EXPLANs for operations-based exercises. The C/E Handbook contains more detailed information about the exercise scenario and guides controllers and evaluators in their roles and responsibilities.

Master Scenario Events List
The Master Scenario Events List (MSEL) contains a chronological listing of the events and injects that drive operations-based exercise play.

Exercise Evaluation Guides
Exercise Evaluation Guides (EEGs) provide evaluators with a checklist of critical tasks to be completed by participants during an exercise. EEGs contain the information to be discussed by participants, space to record evaluator observations, and questions to consider after the exercise.

Activity Background

Objectives

The planning committee continues. The team is working on solidifying objectives.

[Jim, Mary, Paul, Molly, Reese, Josh, and John are sitting at a table]

Jim: Ok, task assignments are done, so let's get down to objectives. Keep in mind; objectives have got to be clear, measurable, and achievable. We're going to be measuring our success against this list – so let's make a good one.

Paul: Well, clearly we've got to have the first arriving agency properly identify that this is a hazardous materials incident. They'll also need to make the appropriate report to the 911 dispatch center.

Molly: I think we'll also have to make sure that the state emergency management director declares a disaster right away.

Reese: Well, back to Paul's point – we'll need the Jonesvillle PD to check in with the IC as soon as they're on the scene. They are going to play a really important part in the transition to a unified command.

Josh: We need to make sure that whoever sets up the IC follows standard operating procedures, calls for assistance, considers evacuation and activation of mutual aid agreements the second this event gets beyond their control.

John: We should make sure the EOC notifies the White House – we want to get the Feds involved in this.

Lesson Summary

You have covered the following topics in Lesson 4:

- Defining Design and Development.
- Assessing Needs.
- Scope.
- Purpose and Objectives.
- Scenarios.
- Exercise documentation.

Lesson 5: Conduct

Lesson Introduction

After completing Lesson 5, you will be able to:

- Describe the differences between discussion and operations-based exercise conduct.
- Understand the basics of discussion-based conduct.
- Understand the basics of operations-based conduct.
- Describe the basic responsibilities of controllers and evaluators.

Lesson Introduction

As you have learned, discussion-based and operations-based exercises differ in their complexity and in their planning processes. There are key differences in how the two types of exercises are conducted as well.

Conduct characteristics differ principally in:

- Time.
- Venue.
- Equipment.
- Number of participants and participant activities.
- Number of planning team members and their activities.

Quick Tip: Operations-based exercises usually require additional logistical considerations such as providing blankets for victim actors in case they have to lie on the ground for a long time, or ensuring that roads will be closed to normal traffic at the exercise venue.

Discussion-Based Conduct

Discussion-based exercise conduct involves:

- Site setup.
- Guided presentation.
- Facilitated/moderated discussion.

- Wrap-up activities.

The majority of discussion-based "action" comes from moderated participant discussions, either as a whole group or in break-out sessions. Moderators and facilitators are essential to keeping the discussions on track to meet exercise objectives.

Setup

- Usually an indoor venue.
- Includes registration, refreshments, identification tags.
- Requires audio/visual equipment and participant tables.

Guided Presentation

- A central tool for facilitating/moderating discussion.
- Usually involves multimedia (with video, sound, and graphics).
- Often used to present scenario narratives (by module).

Facilitated/Moderated Discussion

- Guided discussion aimed at meeting exercise objectives.
- Style varies by exercise type (i.e., formal vs. informal).
- Often led by functional subject-matter experts.

Quick Tip: A facilitator should be an active listener, intervening in the discussion only to guide group activities to ensure that the participants achieve the stated goals and/or objectives of that session. The group must be allowed to collectively reach its own conclusion.

Wrap-Up Activities

- Distributing and reviewing participant feedback forms.
- Conducting a "hot wash".
- Debriefing.

Key Concept: Hot washes are participant feedback sessions immediately following an exercise. They give players a chance to voice concerns and offer potential improvements while the experience is still fresh.

Key Concept: The debrief is a forum for planners, facilitators, controllers, and evaluators to review and provide feedback on the exercise.

These same activities apply for operations-based exercises. The feedback forms, hot washes, and debriefings all provide vital information for the exercise planning team to begin the next stage of the exercise cycle: evaluation.

Quick Tip: Think of the hot wash and debrief as virtually the same thing for different audiences. Hot washes are for players, and occur immediately after the exercise has concluded. Debriefs are for "exercise management" and can take place on the same day or weeks after the exercise.

There are two proven methods of keeping discussions on track:

Facilitated Discussions

- Separate, facilitated group discussions.
- Groups identified by functional expertise.
- Facilitated discussion of scenario and objectives.
- Recorder/notes-taker often present.

Moderated Discussions

- Results of facilitated discussions reported.
- All participants/groups involved.
- Group discussions summarized by group spokespersons.
- All participant discussions controlled by lead moderator.

At times a combination of both styles may be appropriate to use.

Exercise Personnel

Discussion-based exercise personnel include:

- Presenters - Deliver the exercise presentation.
- Facilitators/Moderators - Lead group discussion.
- Controllers - Interpret rules and provide players with information.
- Evaluators - Observe and collect exercise data.
- Players - Discuss issues based on professional knowledge.
- Observers/VIPs - View but do not participate in exercise.

The positions of presenters, facilitators/moderators, and controllers may be combined depending on the size and scope of the exercise.

The conduct of operations-based exercises involves:

- Site setup.
- Exercise briefings.
- Exercise play.
- Wrap-up activities.

The majority of operations-based "action" involves the deployment and use of personnel, equipment, communications, and actual or simulated performance of operations.

Operations-Based Conduct

Site Setup

- Done by the planning team the day before conduct.
- Usually an outdoor venue.

The site setup may include:

- Response Route - routes to the simulated incident.
- Response Area - location of exercise activities.
- Assembly Area - location of deployable resources participating in the exercise.
- Observer/Media Area - designated viewing area.
- Simulation Cell - location generating scenario injects.
- Registration - to ensure only authorized personnel are allowed on scene.
- Parking.

Coordinating logistics is a critical element in operations-based exercise conduct because of the large number of personnel and equipment involved.

Exercise Briefings

- Train and/or inform exercise participants.
- Provide safety information to all personnel.
- Are different for controllers, evaluators, players, and actors.
- Explain exercise play rules (which vary for each exercise).

Wrap-up Activities

- Distribute and review participant feedback forms.
- Conduct a hot wash.
- Conduct a debrief.

Exercise Play Rules

> Key Concept: Exercise play rules describe appropriate behavior for participants when physical contact is necessary or when participants become overemotional or their actions excessive.

Play rules for operations-based exercises are more stringent and formalized because the exercises demand a higher level of intensity from both planners and participants.

Rules are established in advance of the exercise to give participants or actors - such as law enforcement personnel or a barricaded hostage taker - a safety net to prevent physical harm to individuals or damage to property.

Responsibilities of Controller/Evaluator

Controllers and evaluators have two primary responsibilities: keep an exercise on track and assess its performance. Both are essential steps toward capabilities building.

Controllers:

- Plan and manage exercise play.
- Set up and operate the exercise incident site.
- Sometimes simulate non-participating organizations.

Evaluators:

- Track action relative to evaluation objectives.
- Identify any resolved and unresolved issues.
- Help analyze the exercise results.
- Participate in post-exercise meetings and critiques.
- Do not interfere with exercise flow.

Quick Tip: Because of their familiarity with the exercise, planning team members make excellent controllers and evaluators.

Exercise Evaluation Guides

A key document used by evaluators during exercise conduct is the Exercise Evaluation Guide (EEG).

> Key Concept: EEGs provide structured evaluation measures of participant conduct, listing critical activities and tasks to be completed during an exercise. They tell evaluators what they should expect to see, give them space to record observations, and list questions to address after the exercise as a first step in the analysis process.

Some questions an EEG might include:

- Were roles and responsibilities of the various government agencies and private organizations clear?
- How were various decisions made? Who had authority?
- What information about the scenario, the weapon, the victims, and the risks to responders and the public was collected in the course of the exercise?

Quick Tip: Each major emergency response capability identified in the Target Capabilities List (TCL) has its own EEG (e.g. responder safety and health). Which capabilities are being tested and/or evaluated in an exercise will affect how many EEGs evaluators will need.

Activity Background

Conduct

Jim is conducting a player's briefing just prior to the beginning of exercise play.

[Jim is speaking with the players outside at the site of the exercise.]

Jim: Now, in about one hour we'll be kicking off the exercise. As players, you should have had an opportunity to review the Player's Handbook. So before we start the exercise, does anyone have any questions about the exercise assumptions, artificialities, or the Safety Plan?

Steve: Yeah, Jim, what if a real emergency occurs during the exercise.

Jim: Good question, Tom. Did everybody hear Tom's question? Folks, the safety plan covers any Real World Emergency procedures. If, for any reason, an emergency happens during the exercise we will notify any of the control staff immediately. First and foremost, we'll handle the situation. Secondly, we'll leave it to the controllers as to whether we continue to play.

Dan: Now I just want to double check – not all of the ambulances will be evacuating plant workers to the nearest hospitals, right?

Jim: Correct – we'll be transporting about 50 victims via ambulance to Jonesville East and Jonesville West. The other 75 will be triaged, treated, and put on two school busses so we can simulate transport.

Lesson Summary

This lesson covered the following topics:

- Differences between the conduct of discussion-based and operations-based exercises.
- Basics of discussion-based conduct.
- Basics of operations-based conduct.
- Responsibilities of the conduct controller/evaluator.
- Exercise Evaluation Guides (EEGs).

Lesson 6: Evaluation

Lesson Introduction

After completing Lesson 6, you will be able to:

- Describe the methodology used to evaluate an exercise.
- Describe the basic elements of an After-Action Report.
- Identify the eight steps in the evaluation process.

Lesson Introduction

Key Concept: Exercise evaluation assesses how well the exercise objectives were achieved. It also identifies opportunities for improvement.

Evaluators accomplish this by:

- Observing the exercise and collecting supporting data.
- Gauging performance against expected outcomes.
- Determining what changes are needed to ensure desired outcomes.

Evaluation is the yardstick by which an organization measures its capabilities. Good evaluations result in suggestions for filling and bridging capability gaps or making needed improvements.

Quick Tip: Changes might involve an organization's procedures, plans, staffing, equipment, communications, or interagency coordination—or all of these.

Evaluation Methodology

The evaluation methodology of the Department of Homeland Security assesses exercise performance at three levels.

Task Level
The ability of individual players or teams to perform a required task during an exercise.

Organization/Discipline/Functional Level
The ability of an organization (e.g., Jonesville EMA), discipline (e.g., law enforcement), or function (e.g., HazMat response) to perform its role in responding to an event.

Mission Level
The ability of the intergovernmental community as a whole (across disciplines and jurisdictions) to achieve expected outcomes in responding to an event.

Quick Tip: Not every level is assessed in less complex exercises. Discussion-based exercises usually focus on Mission Level issues.

For discussion-based exercises, evaluation focuses on the adequacy of and familiarity with an organization's:

- Plans, policies, and procedures.
- Resources and capabilities.
- Interagency/inter-jurisdictional relationships.

Operations-based exercises often focus their evaluation on areas such as:

- Effectiveness of communications.
- Effectiveness of Incident Command management.
- Ability to properly use equipment.
- Cooperation between agencies.

Evaluation Process

There are eight steps in the HSEEP evaluation process:

Step 1: Plan and organize the evaluation.
The planning team determines what information should be collected, who should collect it, and how it should be collected.

Step 2: Observe the exercise and collect data.
Expert (peer) evaluators gather data by recording their observations during exercise play.

Step 3: Analyze data.
Evaluators analyze:

- Expected versus actual performance.
- Lessons to be learned from conduct.
- Improvements to be made in performance and process.

- Which best practices could be adopted.

Quick Tip: The Exercise Planning Team prepares its evaluation during the design and objectives development process.

Step 4: Develop draft After-Action Report (AAR).
The evaluation team and/or planning team drafts the AAR, a summary of the exercise analysis that:

- Describes what happened during exercise conduct.
- Identifies exemplary practices.
- Highlights issues that need to be addressed.
- Recommends improvements.

Step 5: Conduct After-Action Conference.
The exercise planners and/or evaluation team present their draft AAR to official representatives of exercise participants for feedback and validation.

Quick Tip: The After-Action Conference should always include officials from the agencies and jurisdictions that participated in the exercise.

Step 6: Identify improvement to be implemented.
During the After-Action Conference, planners and evaluators create an Improvement Plan that:

- Identifies the next steps to be taken for improving performance.
- Suggests which individuals, agencies, or organizations should be responsible for implementing the improvements.
- Outlines a timeframe for implementation.

Step 7: Finalize AAR and Improvement Plan.
Planners and/or evaluators incorporate the results, corrections, or clarifications of the After-Action Conference.

Step 8: Track implementation.
Each agency/jurisdiction or organization establishes a process to implement and track its tasks from the improvement plan.

After-Action Reports

The main instrument of exercise evaluation is the After-Action Report (AAR).

> Key Concept: Often prepared by the members of the planning team and evaluation team, the After-Action Report (AAR) provides participant officials with feedback on the exercise's results and suggests recommendations for improvement.

After-Action Reports:

- Should be prepared after every exercise type.
- Summarize what happened during the exercise.
- Provide feedback to participants on their performance.
- Recommend improvements for better preparedness.

> Key concept: A task list and timeline of corrective actions, called the Improvement Plan (IP), is part of the AAR.

Quick Tip: AARs generally include summaries and evaluations of the exercise scenario, player activities, preliminary observations, and major issues.

AARs vary in size and detail, depending on the complexity of an exercise.

Sources for AAR data include:

- Evaluator observation.
- Exercise Evaluation Guides (EEGs).
- Hot wash, debrief, and participant feedback forms.
- Plans and procedures of participant organizations.

> Key Concept: Draft AARs are presented in an After-Action Conference. This forum allows key findings to be aired in a group discussion intended to produce action items for the Improvement Plan.

Quick Tip: The AAR uses organizations' plans, policies, and procedures to compare the actual results with the intended outcome.

Recommended HSEEP AAR Format

> *Executive Summary*
>
> *Exercise Overview*

Includes background information: participating organizations, exercise conduct date and time, location, exercise type, hazard, evaluation methodology.

Exercise Goals and Objectives

Exercise Events Synopsis
Chronological synopsis of major events and actions.

Analysis of Mission Outcomes
Summarizes how the performance or nonperformance of tasks and interactions affected achievement of the mission outcomes.

Analysis of Critical Task Performance
Summarizes and addresses issues regarding each task in terms of consequences, analysis, recommendations, and improvement actions.

Conclusion

Appendix: Improvement Plan Matrix
Provides a task list of recommendations, due dates, and responsible organizations.

Activity Background

Evaluation

Jim is speaking to the exercise participants after the exercise.

[Jim is standing in a large room speaking with exercise participants.]

Jim: Before we wrap up and call it a day, I want to spend maybe an hour conducting the debrief. As most of you know, this debrief is the time set aside for you to give us feedback. We're looking for your initial reactions as to how you think the exercise went.

Mary: I'm going to go around and ask each of the controllers and evaluators in the room to talk about 3 issues you observed during the exercise based on the notes you took and the feedback you received from the players at the Hot Wash. This will help us put together the After-Action Report and Improvement Plan.

Jim: Okay – let's start with the Controller for Incident/Unified Command.

Karl: Yeah, Karl Gray, from Jonesville PD. I got to say the players were a little confused as to the location of the command post – there were no clear markings on the command bus and some of the participants weren't wearing their vests. And I was also concerned about accountability and the lack of communications between agencies.

Jim: Thanks Karl. Okay, now can we get the lead evaluator for IC?

Suzanne: Hi, Suzanne Williams from EMS. I want to put a slightly different spin on what Officer Gray said. As I understand it, one of the key objectives was to have responders check in with command, as soon as they arrived on scene. *Most folks* actually did that. They checked in with command found the command and got there almost immediately. But out in the field, we did find a few people who asked us where it was.

Lesson Summary

This lesson covered the following topics:

- Evaluation Methodology.
- Evaluation Process.
- After-Action Reports (AARs).

Lesson 7: Improvement Planning

Lesson Introduction

After completing Lesson 7, you will be able to:

- Understand the improvement planning process.
- Describe the basics of an After-Action Conference.
- Explain the importance of lessons learned.
- Understand the essentials of implementing an After-Action Report.

Lesson Introduction

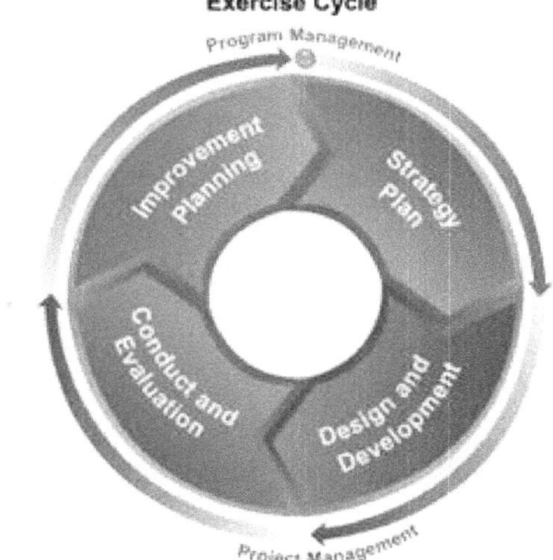

Improvement planning completes the cycle of preparedness that you learned about in Lesson 1.

- Assessments determine which capabilities are needed. Those needs in turn help define:
    - an exercise program's direction and schedule.
    - a strategy for improving training, equipment, and plans.
    - scenarios and objectives for individual exercises.
- Exercises help further assess (and improve) performance.
- Evaluations identify what areas need improving.
- Improvement planning identifies actions designed to ensure improvements are made.

Quick Tip: The goal of DHS is to help jurisdictions and organizations objectively assess their capacity to prevent, respond to, and recover from a disaster, so that modifications or improvements can be made before having to react to a real incident.

The Improvement Planning Process

Key Concept: The Improvement Planning Process is the means for converting recommendations from the After-Action Report (AAR) into measurable steps that, when implemented, lead to improved response capabilities.

By focusing on performance and how actual outcomes differ from expectations, public officials, and exercise planners can:

- Target their improvement resources more effectively.
- Modify their programs before having to respond to a real incident.

This process should be considered a dynamic program that is updated and modified regularly in a constant cycle of improvement.

Pre-Exercise Improvement Planning

Improvement planning should not occur only at the end of an exercise. It can also help shape the planning and design of the exercise.

Because past improvements affect future performance:

- Previous AARs should be referenced early.
- Lessons learned should be incorporated.
- Testing and validation of improvements should be built into the ongoing improvement process.

Understanding how improvements have been handled and completed will affect how an exercise, or exercise program, incorporates the new capabilities.

The Improvement Plan

Key Concept: Organizations execute the improvement planning process using a tool called the Improvement Plan (IP).

The IP identifies:

- Actions to address each AAR recommendation.
- Who will be responsible for taking each action.
- A timeline for completion of those actions.

Once recommendations and action items have been identified, organizations should ensure that each item is tracked to completion and improvements are implemented.

Quick Tip: When no resources are available, alternative short- and long-term solutions such as mutual aid agreements should be considered.

The After-Action Conference

Key Concept: The After-Action Conference, as discussed in lesson 6, is a forum for exercise participants to discuss the draft AAR and identify action items for the IP.

Recommended Conference Attendees:

- Official representatives of all participating organizations.
- Exercise Planners who assisted in the development of the AAR.
- Exercise Evaluators who assisted in the development of the AAR.
- Stakeholders from the city, state, region, or other jurisdictions.

The conference should address:

- Specific improvement actions that agencies can take.
- Feedback and validation of observations and recommendations.
- Key lessons learned from the exercise experience.
- Distribution of the After-Action Report (AAR) and the Improvement Plan (IP).

The After-Action Conference

The Improvement Plan Matrix

During the After-Action Conference, attendees often use an Improvement Plan Matrix to finalize the AAR/IP.

It includes:

- Tasks.
- Recommendations.
- Improvement Actions.
- Responsible Party (Parties).
- Completion Date.

Tasks in the matrix should match those from the Exercise Evaluation Guides, while recommendations and improvement actions should be taken from the body of the After-Action Report.

Below is an example of an Improvement Plan Matrix.

Tasks	Recommendations	Improvement Actions	Responsible Party	Due Date
III-14 Provide emergency public information to the media and the public	1. Emergency Management Agency (EMA) should establish procedures or protocols to ensure that news releases reach all affected counties or agencies, regardless of their Emergency Management System capabilities.	1. The director of EMA will issue a directive requiring that all personnel assigned to work in the Joint Information Center (JIC) receive a copy of the operating procedures, become familiar with them, and follow them during an emergency.	EMA Director	May, 2006
		2. The director of EMA will convene a working group with representatives from selected counties to develop a plan to provide all counties with access to the EMS and to train county staff.	EMA Director	June, 2006

Implementing the AAR

Within your community, try to determine the best way to share lessons learned from exercises and actual incidents. This could entail maintaining a library of AARs, a list in the Emergency Operations Center (EOC), or your community's own secure website.

Lessons Learned
The building block approach to preparedness relies on lessons learned from earlier efforts - in exercises, training, policies, and procedures - and communication of those lessons.

- AARs identify lessons learned and improvements.
- Those lessons not communicated will be lost.
- Sharing lessons enhances preparedness nation-wide.

DHS has created a Lessons Learned and Information Sharing (LLIS) network to collect and disseminate best practices identified during exercises and actual incidents (available at https://www.llis.dhs.gov/user/login). To maximize the value of an exercise, planners are encouraged to share the lessons learned and best practices on this secure network.

Managing the Implementation

Implementing the recommendations from the AAR and action items from the IP can be complex and may require significant resources and funding. Not every suggested improvement may be achievable. With this in mind, planners should:

- Prioritize according to benefits rather than costs.
- Use local resources as much as possible.
- Have a solid method for monitoring improvements.
- Regularly review improvement progress.
- Review potential alternatives if progress is not being made.

Simply by tracking improvements, exercise participants may identify additional needs and tasks. Roadblocks to achieving improvements may also highlight issues not previously recognized.

Quick Tip: At the very least, reviews of improvement progress should occur at the Exercise Planning Workshop (EPW), when the Multiyear Plan is created.

Activity Background

After-Action Reports/Improvement Planning

Jim is conducting the After-Action Conference. As the Lead Planner, Jim reads out the Critical Task Performance findings from the AAR. The team is then putting together the Improvement Plan.

[Jim and the participants are sitting in a large room.]

Jim: Alright, now for the fun part. We're going to take the next half hour to fill in our Improvement Plan Matrix. [Jim is pointing to a chart] This chart is going to serve two purposes for us. Number one: gives us a clear understanding of areas we need to improve upon. And, number two: gives us a plan with action items, due dates, and responsible parties attached, to achieve those improvements.

Mary: Essentially, we'll be taking the key issues identified and agreed upon in the AAR – which you all have in front of you [The planners look at their AARs] – and we're going to put those findings in the improvement plan matrix. By doing so we'll be able to identify which agency among you will be responsible for making the identified changes and determine a timeline for each task to be completed.

Jim: For example, the AAR said that the location of our command post wasn't clear. So one of our action items should be to clearly mark the Command Post Bus and purchase some vests for the Command Staff.

Lesson Summary

This lesson covered the following topics:

- The improvement planning process.
- The basics of an After-Action Conference.
- The importance of lessons learned.
- The essentials of implementing an After-Action Report.